Call of the Void

Call of the Void

Brian R. Strauss

Chula Vista, California

A **SWOLLEN APPENDICES** Publication

978-0-9963221-2-6

Acknowledgments

To Mom and Dad for making me feel safe enough to take risks as a human, as an artist, and as crazy as they are (truly insane humans) they've always made me feel like the only option was to be myself.

To Mrs. Demangos from high school who first encouraged me to consider English as a major in college, who showed me the poetic meter of *Light My Fire* by The Doors and ultimately lead me to become a poet.

To Gillian Conley who in college gave me the courage and guidance to become a practiced and disciplined poet.

To Christian who used to let me read early drafts of these poems to him in his backyard late into the night while giving thoughts on what worked and what didn't.

To the friends I've lost—who have all in some way informed the way I approach writing, or the processing of grief and love, or who taught me how to peel away the anger from others to find the vulnerability hiding beneath. I love and miss each of you so much even all these years later.

To the numerous underground lit mags who published some of these poems years before I ever put them in book form, many of whom have defaulted and whose names I could no longer find.

If you have ever been a friend to me, thank you. I don't think I'd be capable of handling this world were it not for the kindness of so many people in my life.

Words About *Call of the Void*

"Brian R. Strauss' *Call of the Void* is a work of experimental and original verse. Each page is its own experience of story poem. One does not simply read Strauss' collection and tuck the book away for the night; instead, it ignites sensation and true reflection with its imagery of broken glass, the flame from a lighter that dances, or the flapping wings of a fly."

–Briana Muñoz,
   Author of *Everything is Returned to the Soil*

"Brian Strauss' poetry is like a drunken walk home while the rest of the world sleeps: lusty, romantic, and sad. *Call of the Void* contemplates the ethereal qualities of love and language, which Strauss can render as cages or wings, depending on the mood. Despite how many one-night stands, sordid adventures and unrequited romances drip from these pages, a passion for words is the real love story here."

–Ryan Bradford
   Founder of AwkSD

Foreword

It's been about six and a half years since I put out my first collection of poems, *Call of the Void*. In that time, I put out another collection of poetry about a year later and the five years since I've written sporadically, but I largely put writing aside in favor of music. Every few months I'd churn out a few short poems, but after having written so often for so long, I was feeling burnt out. It wasn't just the writing though, life was tumultuous. Rather than continue to process those feelings, I chose to go deep into my professional career and into music. There was camaraderie in both that I didn't have in writing. I've never felt a part of any artistic community which is odd since I pop into so many local shows and so many local readings, nonetheless I've always felt like I'm watching from the outside.

So why now? After all these years I've finally sat down and done some reappraising of my work. It began last year in October 2020 when I was holed up with my brother in our parents' little Wyoming house. It was just he and I, and there was too much snow to go anywhere or be outside except for the occasional cigarette, and so we'd each work remotely for the day and at the end of the workday we'd share a few shots of whiskey and have dinner together. He started work at 6am and I'm an early riser regardless so while he'd be in his office making calls, I'd sit at the kitchen table watching the snowfall and drinking my coffee. I got to reading while I drank my coffee in the mornings and about two weeks into our four weeks there, I started to write.

It came quickly. There were a lot of pent-up thoughts I'd been sitting on for a while and I wrote more in those two weeks than I'd written in the last three years at least. So, when it was time for us to finally leave Wyoming, I'd written something along the lines of thirty-five poems, which doesn't seem crazy until you realize this book is forty-one poems. Also it's important to remember I hadn't done much writing in the last half decade. Then I got back to my apartment in Dallas where through the month of November I churned out another twenty-five thousand words of a novel. I was in a whole mood, the flood gates had been opened, and my chardonnay budget was ballooning.

But this is not about inspiration, it was about becoming a practiced and disciplined artist again. I did it with music for so long, and in my professional life as a marketer. It was deeply cathartic to fall back into writing as a craft especially years later with a much more studious approach. And so this is where the reappraisal began, I started to look back at my earlier work. Much of *Call of the Void* had been written during my final year and a half in college in Northern California. And it shows in my willingness to use such varied and experimental forms, but also in how it lacked a certain polish and consistency.

The writing itself is visceral and written with such youthful intensity and I remember writing many of the poems under intense conditions often under tight time constraints. There's another side to that though, which is that youth can often bring a less refined talent. In the first edition there are scores of formatting errors and inconsistencies, many of which I use purposefully in the poems themselves, but that the average reader wouldn't be able to distinguish from just a good ol' fashioned gen-u-ine fuck up. I fixed a lot of the quality control issues when I put out my follow-up *Strung Like Puppets*, but it still left my debut suffering. And there's a lot of goodness in this collection that I just felt like I could really do better justice to all these years later, especially as I reacquaint myself with writing as an art form.

The other component beyond quality control is that I've made lots and lots of edits. Taking the time to sit with these poems and ruminate on what they mean, how they can be interpreted, and how I shape those interpretations has been something I've thought deeply about for several reasons: One reason was my youthful inclination towards being somewhat of a pseudo-provocateur. What I mean with this is I was a bit too liberal with my foul language. Not that there's a problem with cursing in poetry, there's still plenty of that in here, but the purpose in using the language that I do has never been to offend, which unfortunately is what some readers have taken away, but has been to reflect the taxonomy of these very real scenes and environments (real in the sense they reflect real life not that these are true stories).

As a side bar I'd like to remind everyone that "I" in poetry is very different from "I" in real life. Writing from the first-person does not make the speaker "Brian Strauss." These poems are N E V E R told from my perspective, because they are not me. The speaker is the speaker, the character, the fiction that has been created. Their actions reflect their narratives, not mine personally, and that distinction is important for me to establish.

People use unpleasant language, oftentimes outright prejudicial language towards others. There are scenes in this collection that reflect that reality. That is an unfortunate component of life. Even more unfortunate is in the intervening years since I published the first edition of *Call of the Void* language as discourse has become on the whole more vitriolic. I'm a half indigenous-Latino and half white man, so I've always had a somewhat complex relationship to race and gender in the context of self-identity. Was I being bold? Or was I being a prick? Is it prejudiced to illustrate prejudice? I don't believe so, however I also don't believe I always hit the mark in terms of the nuance needed to effectively convey those themes. In those instances, I have made edits to reflect those inadequacies and to reflect how my relationship and understanding of that dialogue has evolved.

"You inspired me to cuss more in my own poetry," a fellow writer once told me to my disappointment. Because then purpose ceases to exist and they're just ugly "extraneous ornaments" as Quiller-Couch would say.

That's a problem because my poetry is supposed to be accessible. It's layered for the academics, but it's also meant to be enjoyed and to resonate with readers. People should see a part of themselves in art, but if they feel as though art is actively rejecting them, then we've lost the plot. Ultimately that's what compelling art is: it's a reflection of the people who engage it and ideally it at times reflects parts of themselves that they weren't even aware of.

Art does not change the world (despite what many artists claim) but it does change people. It reminds us to be present, to be mindful of both our surroundings and what we take from it, in how we treat others, and in how we treat ourselves. I've done my best to ensure this new edition of *Call of the Void* serves to provide a more nuanced demonstration of life's beauty, its sorrow, its cruelty, and its fickle nature. It is a book that challenges readers to confront the intimacy of personal love and trauma–all of its turmoil, conflict, and the glimmers of joy and triumph that punctuate our lives. At the very least I hope you get an enjoyable afternoon read out of it in a park on the grass with the sun out and a bottle mid-shelf port to quench your thirst.

Thanks for reading,

B. Strauss

To Stefany.

Poems

Man Gives You a Cup of Coffee, Take a Sip

Thick beard that seems to callous his anxious face,
A tender nervousness permeates his expression.
Delicate drags of my cigarette that linger from his lips
As he pulls the fag away-   Arms outstretched then.

Beside me another, slick haired, fast-talker with a rolling
Sort of speech the way his tongue stumbles over itself to
Push syllables out of his mouth. Parliament between lips.

Coffee cup sits on table, vapor lifting, still full-
Man gives you a cup of coffee, take a damn sip
, he says.

So the beard smiles through the hairs fondling his face and
says he did.

No you didn't, slick replies, seizing the cup for himself.
        'f you won't drink it, I will.

I light another cigarette, handing one to the beard as I do.
You're as ugly as you look, I think
Reflection in the handle of the rail beside me- Smiling
placidly.

What is more important, he asks me,
        The poet or the poem?   It depends on the
nature of the poem.

The poem. The work should stand as its own.

Both wrong answers. It is the nature of
the poet that matters.
There's a right answer?

Flicks cigarette ash into receptacle-   cold flame burning
beneath bit knuckled white
Exclamatory gestures of poetic parables, he's preaching the
good word of unfold notepad
Forget   ful, nature that it is.

Hollow, vapid, emptiness: synonyms
Which is to say that he's a dull boy
Kind of looks a bit the part if it weren't for the fact that it's
fashionable now.

Words beating themselves over the head with concrete
bricks
Immense in density, hallow emptiness pervades itself.

I do not mean empty when I mean horrifying,
But the two coalesce in his case.

Lilac looking eyes, that's all.
This is Mia, frolicking in finagled fungus, constantly
condoning consonance,
Thick brush of curls sprouted from her scalp, con-cave
cheeks seductively
Begging me,

With obtrusive eyes bulging loudly from her skull,
Mismatched against the speck of her voice. Small,

characteristically deep ridge
in her left cheek, probably a scar.   Unlike ring that
pierces right nostril.

Smoke trails off tips of her lips, she's burying fags in piles of
ashed monuments
Marble-esque eyes, olive skin basking in the luminary
ambience of evening light.
Meandering gaze split me intwo-   I thought I'd
stay a young man
Forever.

Hair thins way lips purse together- fearfully wrinkle up
Look at her laughing at the shape of his skull, head so big
I'd like to kiss it before thumping it inward
Shattered mess of ash and porcelain.

I'd told him I was gonna use that line, the one about coffee
He shifts in his seat but I ignore him-   After a long silence
he finally speaks up,

   It's not a big deal, but when you take something it's polite
to ask.

He looks sharply, offendingly at me.
I can only laugh.

Supermoon

I've been thinking in accents lately.

There's this fly on the floor next to me here at work,
the flapping of his tiny little wings
buzzing against the floor
becoming more and more languid every time I
return.

I've gotten in the habit of looking through things
rather than at them.
Perpetually,
Well–it's more than dreaming.

I almost crashed my car yesterday evening on my way to
work.
My head was just not in the right place.

I seem to be distracted
most of the time these days.

Outside there's a dull roar
Emanating from behind clouds blanketing dusk sky
obscured cosmic figures of abnormal prominence,

I keep imagining a tidal wave
sweeping away everything–me included
which is strange since I had a dream last night
where I was swimming under water through the bushels of
seaweed

I didn't need to breathe,

I just felt the weightlessness of floating
quietly among the throngs of brightly colored fish

swimming by in their segregated schools
several of them–each for a moment

resting in my hand as if I might carry them along with me
that space-like tranquility

lingering.

That fly is still buzzing.
Maybe I ought to put him out.

Christ

Days drone on like merciless small talk
Ears penetrated by gilded words
Words counting the missteps of words
Seeding themselves fixed upon their reflections
Of lowly creatures ensnared within the traps
Of indignant proclivities
rolling eyes smothering thoughts of entitled
greatness

Pretentiousness presides beneath the sun-spotted
skin of breaded Christ-like bodies
Offering themselves up on pedestals of flesh
Drenched in salivating wine
Licking the lips of tender looking virgins
Hoping for a kiss but forego the
disappointment.

Lilac looking envy of blonde haired prince
Cobalt looking eyes Marlboro sharpened tongue
Whiskey coated breath ginger-tipped beard
Eyes looking coldly out beyond the scenery
Of pleasant desert oasis gilded decadence

What a fucking bore, he says to me
And I can only lay there plain-faced and grim
Bubbling anger obscured beneath a control
Codeine complacency numbing the boiling tension
The warming sadness of inconsequential arguments
Only feeding the lingering sensation of dissatisfaction
With the company one keeps

With the company of long-haired men
With broken hearts and stagnant minds
And set ways
And rotting livers
And suffocating lungs
Drowning in his own words
Fragmented thoughts copulating
With a passionate fury that once was
More than just talk but became inadequate
That became the greatest disappointment
of my life (yet)

Nonetheless,
here I sit
sipping whiskey on my coke
entranced by the liquor on my breath
and the smoke leaving my lungs
and the broken glass beneath my feet
Digging like his words eat my soul
Like his glare singes my wounds
And I think aloud as I drive my car
back home every night and some mornings
Speaking to his empty passenger seat
Why
And I ask
And again once more
Endlessly asking
never knowing
Never caring
If only.

Eyes Without a Face

((O))

People have this tendency to look outward through the
corners of their eyes
Rather than straight on-   makes a big
difference.
When you're looking at someone from the edge of your
peripherals
It becomes difficult to notice when their pupils widen with
interest,
When their glance wanders past you,
When their brow furls in contempt,
When their face becomes a colorful canvas silently begging
your attention.

It's midnight in the city,

Downtown everything is still open, so I sit in an all-night
cafe
Sipping coffee smoking cigarettes, save for the vanity of
eyes
I'd have stayed home, but it doesn't feel that way anymore.
I think about using knife wounds as extra pockets
  -Thought remains incorrigible.

Inside there is warmth, but everyone is carefully observing
each other
Pretending not to see the carefully fired glances that shoot
their way.

My heart breaks a million times over with each.

There's a sort of spell the glance puts one under,
It is an addictive substance salivating lust in the heart
But not the brain. You know better.

Better get to work...I might think to myself
At some point in the night.

I don't enjoy the glamorized portrayal of sleeplessness,
Nor the feelings it invokes.

Even on nights like these I remember there aren'
t enough left, so I try not to let it bother.
Try to think of as gift, makes it easier.
There are no easy days though,
Only long ones.

Days stitched together way nights are sewn together
Time quilted into pictures like manuscripts begging to be
read.

At least lines are never uniform.

I can see out the window of the cafe that
There are many cars with headlights on, and bicycled riders
Riding for three, for four, sometimes five,
Carriages being carried through traffic.

It might rain, but my car is around the corner
Tenderly sleeping until I return, patiently waiting
Forever.
There is too much emphasis on the singularity of word

It escapes me, similar to my understanding of chess.

Strategy has never been my strong suit.

Then I guess you'd want to know what's at stake,
What I have to lose, you always do,
And it wouldn't surprise me if with stifled breath you're
standing over my shoulder
Waiting for me to praise your holiness, the way you half-
heartedly feign humility
Expectant and indignant.

And then of course there's the woman.

I'm looking out the corners of my eyes at this handsome
young man
Sitting there, strange glow about it as he reads his book.
Ginsberg- as they always do, anyways
He's got this nest of ruffled red feathers with dark brooding
ponds for eye caverns
Beneath his table is a leather bag with whiskey bottle neck
sticking out enthusiastically.
I feel myself laughing.
His eyes are stiff with avoidant awareness.
This only makes me laugh more loudly, my eyes staring
direct upon him as I do.
Stood up, slinging the bag-strap over his shoulder, looking
at the ground as
Walked out.

My father was a shipyard worker with a knack for craftiness.
My mother always said he was the type of man who could
have saved us on the Titanic through his own volition. I was

obliged to believe it.

When I was a small child he built a scale replica of his
childhood home for us in the backyard to play in.

Outside cafe redhead stands smoking cigarette with eyes
wanting to be watched.
When I step out into the cold it bites at my nose. I light a
cigarette. Eye contact.
We're in an alley, I'm ramming it in.

Back in the cafe it's warm.
It seems like the type of place that would have a fireplace. I
always wished I could find a cafe with a fireplace.
Something serene about staring into the fire, even if after a
while when you're too close it starts to burn the eyes.

There's a drum beat playing itself over and over again in my
mind
An incessant loop, ulterior and motivated   My heart's
got the inkling to dance.
Black boots with rips in the leather, still shiny enough to
glisten in the wetness of the streets
Beneath skies canvassed in maroon and copulating
moonlight.
Moon itself hung like flower from mantle.
Sky used to be the only one who knew the resonant
frequency of clouds.

My favorite bum sets up just around the corner from the
cafe
Hand out for some cash,
I always tell him he better use it for a good drink.

[13]

He says, Only the best, Steel Reserve!
And we both have a good laugh about it, I'll usually give
him some cigarettes too for good measure.

I pull two shooters from my pocket and down each one
before walking into the club.

((O)) ((O))

My favorite part about the club is just how careless
everyone seems to be.
Extravagance of the music, the lights, the dancefloor, the
people welded together at crotch and mouth
Bottles popped wildly, patrons scrambling to let loose
golden foamy rivers of indulgence
Lines being railed off tables and tits, body shots, cigarettes,
bathroom fuckery
Way lights flicker madly enough to incite epileptic fits,
spread of colors blurred, coupled with the blurriness of
poor vision, darkness, and drunken stupor
I stand there at the bar for a while before this girl starts
talking to me
Real sweet smile the way it curves upward, digging into her
cheek, little row of teeth glowing under the lights
There isn't much distance between as we yell at each other,
trying to hear ourselves think an impossibility to begin with
But it brings our mouths closer into contact until I can feel
her breath on my lips, warmth of her skin so close it
emanates onto mine
Eyes glossed over like marbles dipped in porcelain;
Shiny, bulging, luminescent

It isn't long before we're back with her group of friends
laughing over jokes none of us can hear and we're
collectively jumping, shooting tops off with a loud POP!
Foam exploding out over everyone in the crowd as I shake
the bottle with my thumb pressed over the mouth
Some guys try to get in on our party and there's one in
particular getting handsy with my woman so I sit down in
our booth watching him try at it until she gets bold and
begins yelling obscenities at him
She sits down with me, close enough that our legs and
shoulders are touching, and she begins to run her fingers up
and down my arm
I grab her by the hand and she follows me out to the
parking lot where we kiss for a little bit before security asks
us to leave the premises if we aren't going inside
I pull out two shooters, but she politely declines and tells
me she's going back in with her friends. I put them away
and walk back towards the cafe, passing by my favorite
bum. No luck tonight? Not tonight, I mutter back at him,
solemn and morose.

$$((O)) \ ((O)) \ ((O))$$

The cafe had cleared out.
Emptiness can always be felt-   . Waitress
stands behind counter writing something down
I think about what she must be writing.
pores   in my thoughts breathing lubricant

Emptiness is pervasive,   and asymmetrical.
I have the waitress bring me a hookah. I watch her set it up,

[15]

a malignant sense of awareness overtakes her and she drops
    coal trying to light. Burns right through
    cushioning of seat. I poured coffee on it   .
She seems somewhat relieved.

But there is no attraction on her part.

have her bring me a cup of mexican coffee to replace one I
poured out. pour a shooter into it-   have her bring me
more cinnamon.
feels like dry gags when I inhale, my breath tingling my
throat, I ask for a cup of water.
It doesn't bother me that I'm being needy and I don't think
it bothers her actually. There's something that tells me she
feels safe with someone else in here.

        That's a pathetic fallacy if I ever heard one.
It's getting late, but I'm not ready to go   ,just yet.

So I finish my coffee and leave a good tip. I walk along the
road, wishing for the warmth of the cafe, the excitement of
the club, the camaraderie of my undersheltered friend.
When I stumble back over to the club, people are beginning
to leave, and at the side of the building I can see a cop car
parked with its lights flashing. I keep my distance, but I can
see some poor fool perched against the back of the squad
car, sweating beer and pissing profanity from the porous
tastebuds of his face.

   Officer stops to look around before jamming black-
clubbed extremity into swollen gut parched with liquor and
sweat, sweet smell of nightly kerosene. Teeth glinting about
like crazed luminary coal miner's shovel, picking the axe

that might fall upon a transient drunken head. Finger's fondling inseam, keeping eyes at proper distance.

Car pulls out; driving among the herded metallic tons. I pull a cigarette from my pack, hand shaking beneath the quiver of the flame that's dancing about attempting to fornicate the tip of my fag. I figure it's time to go home.

Guess I ought to get to work then.

Ache

Perforated mindslots punching cards like time

Punches wounds
That itch with uncertain futility
Ache - Ache - Aching
In regression
Recoiling arms shriveled stems collapsing inward
An implosive outreach
Extended on beyond paralyzed paraplegic pussy-pushers
Staaaaining themselves with pity sex that began
As thieved kisses plucked up like daisies
Behind black luxury sedans
At funerals on Tuesday mornings when everyone should be
at work
But they're working on themselves and they're working on
each other
Hunched over keyboards in their cubicles
Slouching towards IKEA ordering lampshades out Roebuck
catalogs
Lathering their stomach linings with fat swine
All the while,

Waiting for the day you die
Of stomach or pancreatic cancer
After you lost your foot to diabetes
And the coyotes eat your corpse

,starting with your asshole.

Solidarity of Solitude

I'm going to the beach today
I want to be alone.
  Alone at the beach on a summer day in San Diego?

 Right.

You have no idea.

The low murmurs of a crowd in motion
Endlessly chattering laughing yelling
Herds groaning about happily
Sort of listless liveliness
Oxy-morons never reaching out
Only holding on to what's there

Who's out there in the cold abyss of
Beach junkie phobioatic timers
Ricocheting rockets
Lingering behind piled treestump vomit
Colored brightly lit neon orange lights
Mardi gras deforestating

Funicular Intaglio
Lettered soonglasses
Telling everything you need to know
For ten bucks at the meatswap
And a two-pack of gum that tastes like
Cigarette mouthwash

What the hell are you talking about I say to him

Or I meant I asked him,

It's so convoluted by the time it comes out
he says,
That you've missed it.

Missed what?

    Everything.

Swimming Alongside Venus

I had a dream we were swimming again
I had a dirty dream
Lucky you

She winked at me
And smiled.

Maybe
 I just don't know when to take a hint.

Hawaiian shorts and shirtless
Finite belly loose strands of hair sprouted around nipples
My nipples not hers to be clear
Hula for me baby

Understated outfit
With maskless face spouting jokes to ease the tension
Hair tangled in knots from not washing
From salted emerald waves foaming over delicate figure
Cloaked in dark rubber suit, zip me she says
Turning her back towards and looking at me from the
corner of her eye

I slid my fingers up her neck as I did.

Tender giggle at sight of me in short shorts
Body-pressed-against
How've you been
And the answer's always the same.

Stepping towards the edge of shore
On a lonely afternoon
Soft sound of water sloshing against rocks nearby

She's always in the back of my mind and the tips of my ears
Nagging in jealousy wondering aloud if I fucked her
Much less wondering and much more accusing.
All I can do is smile and say no darling,

We only swam.

Layne Barrett Kind of Girl

In the crazy way she is, like the toad slopping off the backstoop afraid to break a few bones, but not enough to not. Double negative positrons makes for a positively enthralling conduit of self-expression, as a means of self-expression. Licking at the ends of braceful endurance, slopping about cathartically morose and substaining on substance that meanders the monumental movement of glacially paced freedmens. She lacks the kind of will ya look for in the worldly sort of loop, loping itself frontward and backways towards a slouched serenity. Really it comes down to whether it equates itself with that primordial backache that requires surgery on the stegmatta, legmatta, eggmatta, frattatta, gelatta, mulatta, mymamma in a sauna bawse. You know what you're talkin' about, trust you. Don't be unafraid to say what you don't mean because what the haven does it mean to mean nonsense anywho? Sleeping on schoolbuses but nobody's quietly cheering except down dancehalls that burned up moments before tomorrow's last year. Coat it in a prime lacquer and bet you it doesn't clean up like you wish it wouldn't, but it will anyhow because doesn't it always break that way, or at least break me?

Faded Modernity

take advantage of the madness while it persists. you can't
stifle voices so deeply embedded in culture and habit-   a
beautiful thought, lingers about the cortex, how cerebral.
drop me a line so i can drop it further. i'm not tiring, i'm
persistent, i'm walking on transparent chicken wire, cooped
up in declarative run ons long streaming thoughts of parallel
possibilities. release me from the rhythms of inadequate
language foreboding the failings of consequential truths.
speaking thickly the way women dance bodily and
forthright- clumsy male movements

blocks of linguistic perspiration stimulate the simulation of
refracting light splintered across my vision. i see what you
did there- laying it all out for me like that. i'm not so simple
to think myself brilliant only lazily induced sleeplessness, a
recurrent day dozed off. there's no camaraderie you know in
the flintlicked pedestals of sacrifical oaths- they take hand
wipes to clean the blood off- cause they don't then it gets to
a drip- drip-ing outoward the stationary pencil maker
cutting away flesh and vitriolic gel- retinal detachment

you can't stifle voice-only what it says.

there's a difference in being benign and cancerous. where's
your sense of narrative anymore
it seems it's disappeared with the motivation behind it- has
it become so straining to maintain plot or is it only an
aesthetic nuisance
                 it's an ungainly seething of teeth gnashed together
like broken porcelain- divided merely by dashes of

exuberant confidence- dashing away plights of oratory
philosophy
manage to stay quiet in a crowded library as the perpetuated
streaks of purple cry laughter

                          does it suggest an animate object,
lazeye enough susan thought not ought to   trying to play
with words the way yused to but it's an absentia art
salivating in its own drowning of   -don't ask what it is-
            abstract thoughts remain inexplicable save for
permafrost sensation permanency of chil

            drenched apathy- in what little remains.

pAn(I)mosity

Ran the light, cop behind follows closely but after a
moment airy (laps of fear) he speeds by on his great white
bike on the prowl for some thing bet her something moore
inte-resting thana couple of kids speeding pastal toes down
Revolucion. Who are we but a couple of dumb foreigners
feigning indigeny? Let the bar tender slyde the drink over to
you with a cool confidence like you haven't
scene
 in a while
accept from prostitutes in those sleazy backdoor hotels with
the vi be r ating beds we all tried to use as kids (if you've
ever spent your chiled hood in those types of places). Never
really knowing what the hell is going on just that some thing
is going on some ware... think about that
 necks time
   you are master baiting and I guarantee you something will
stand erect. There's probably some poor Dog s lie ding in N
out of alley ways getting picked up in the mid dull of the
after nuncas no one cares enough to say anything so they
don't even bother trying to hide it beneath the cask aiding
dark Ness.
 wait in line wait in line wait in line wait in line wait in line
wait line wait line wait in line wait in line wait in line wait in
line.
Bye, the food, try to speak, he has no clue, only words he
gets: Seen your buried toe? so he gives it to me and I realize
I didn't wash my hands after I got piss all over them in the
street while I walked on the high way but traffic sso slow
I'm walking and pissing beside the car as it rolls on Children
holding pup/pies in the air trying to cell them, some one

[26]

tells me the burrito I ate was made from cat or Dog meat.

 but
I don't care much cause it was the best damned buried toe I
ever had, I swear to God.

Then I get to thin king bout the massage parlor I was in
 how cheap happy endings are there
May be
 Eye lull
go back. Not like I have the time to talk anyways, I'm busy
doing other things, busy thinking a bout where I'll be in 5
years. I used to think it was so stupid the way people could
let themselves end up alone but now I just laugh cause it's
true how easy it is to end up
 On your Own.
That bar was real nice, some hotel my sister's friend owns
so the drinks were on him.
    absinthe, tastes like black licorice.
Order a whiskey, stray tuh, the girl next to me's gagging
from the smell but I order her a Chivas anyways.
She smiles
and her arm slides over my hand
  past my wrist
    up to my neck
and next thing I know she's on top of me in that sl-easy hoe
tell down the road with the bed vye
bray ting and now it all makes cents to me why it's for ah
dults own lee
an eye-mm
loving loving loving loving loving it all, absolutely.

Wonder if I'd make a good Fa(r)ther.

[27]

I burst i burst i burst i burst i burst iburst iburst eyeburst
IBURST!
Purl nek less. Dar
ling let me inside again, but she's tuh eye erd
an
passed out so I leave her there to pay the bill cause I don't
really have the money. I go back to the bar and the tee veez
are all on playing fu'tbol or foot-ball or what-ev-er the hell it
is yore in tu.
They always love the ring, lotta Latin fighters in the ring and
they love the anima(I)city that's just how they are, how we
are. They gotta throw sum blud into the micks otherwise
things get terribly dull extremely fast, that s just the nature
of things. Can- toh nuh gun, byuh .44 mag numb for shhh-
its an gih guls, fire that sucker off and wah ch- the blue
flame burst out the tip a that gat like a han tryna catch its
seed be for it s outta reech.
Bursting bursting bursting bursting
I wrote a letter asking her if she loves me, maybe she'd
want to come with me, I haven't heard back. Fingers
crossed,
May be...It's just blind hopefulness.
(I) can feel it already. This aint wormwood is it? He smiles
and keeps cleaning his glass with that filthy white rag of his,
or at least it was white, maybe, some time ago.
Say my name, whats my name, say my name, say my
name, say my
name what the hell is wrong with you, stop that relentless
shaking it s freeking me the hell out
I justw atnw a another drink for goodssenakesss.
Pleasurable pleasureable pleasure able?
calm. calm calm calm

Whiskey one ice cube. Shot of tequila with Tabasco in it.
Burns so good.
Light
 a cigarette cause thank God you can still burn one here in
the bars and restaurants. itsa fucking miracle I tell you.
 forget about it.. forget about it but that bitch from the
hotel just came
 down and she's pissed, how'd she know to find me-
he(a)re?

i don't trust a woman like that,

  where's my wallet? front pocket who does that?
intelligent people of course who wouldent like getting
pickpocketed in this Godforsaken place. Thatid be just
great. the rest of your family looks white but you're the
token beaner looking motherfucker. Those icey
sonsofbitches will probably think iam being smuggled
across the border. HA! I problee speak better ing lish than
most of those motherfuckers!
  Somehow at some point somewhere I traded my twenty
for two hundred pesos and some drinks. Flashes of a man
buying me a bucket of beer, every woman I met was named
Guadalupe or at least I thought so and I may have been
ripped off. Theres a chip in my front tooth and my family is
absolutely furious.
  What do they expect, young guy like me let loose in this
orgy of hedonism....
(hee hee hee haa haa haa!)
ime bound tu mayk a few mis takes, orso ive ben tot thru
my x ten siv life x peer ee inse.
(hee hee hee haa haa haa!)
 Doe nt stress a bout it thoe, giv em tie mmm, thay ll ferr

[29]

get, or thay ull...
or they'll turn it into a joke and
 (hee hee hee haa haa haa!)
all of a sudden you're that hilarious sonofabitch
   (hee hee hee haa haa haa!)
who does crazy shit like that.

Hee hee hee Ha Ha Ha Ha
HAAAA!

And I turn
and say to mother,

smiling as only I smile

How bout that?

Giant

Fleas are like giants the way they fondle threads of grass like flesh feels fur, like coins feel slots punched out like back alley drunken barroom brawls. I'm lying by the river of disease and I can feel that I'm dying, not really, but Jesus and Mary tell me so. Words are not ethereal, but they are redundant which I guess is important if you're into sordid displays of unequivocal imbalance, chemical malice, but in the way a pie might deflate after you take it out of the basket. Do you understand that I'm not addressing you when I say I am- Saving questions like pockets fill change. There's a crab that plucks out eyes like livers pluck brandy from the quarter of your tongue, so silvery blonde in that strawberry flavor I love. That you love to say I love anyhow. What's an accordion without line, it's an unwound throng of pedestrians molesting each other with delightful anguish. Don't bother language the way it bothers itself to have made, just make, just-ify. Told a flower once he was a he, but really who knows. I mean someone knows, but who, they don't know. So we'll just go with that for then.

The Meat Rack

High top sneakers on the feet of a queer walking by cutting
rubber with each step.

Strange-
like gracefulness to the stride though, almost floating
above the stony lamplit path.

Some spick, dancin' in the moonlight
thinks he's real hot-shit the way
he moves his feet, really shuffles those fuckers,
glaring up at me with a flirtatious snark.

Light a cigarette; watch the smoke trail off like a
silvery bloodletter reflecting against the droplets of light
that hadn't completely washed away from the sky
as the moon perched itself high above the edge of reason.

Slide my hand across the table, gently over hers
and feel that warmth emanating, a hot coal in my grasp.
Give her the chance to pull back, then hard and firm,
remember you're a man. Act accordingly.

Look at the way she fiddles with her hair,
the way she chews her nails, and looks at her feet.
Take notice of her nervously biting the corner of her lip,
tender pink pillows, luscious and moist.

That little spick's still there swayin' his hips
like pendulums of flesh swinging
to some unheard pulse, some soundless rhythm.

Keep your eye on the girl, lean in close.

Don't jump the gun though. Pull back and light another
cigarette, make her really want it, let her build it up
in her own mind. You won't disappoint, you know that.
You're just... looking for a bit of attention.

Preten(d)se

Why don't you love me?
If you won't love me, at least fuck me
For godssakes I'm starved in a kennel somewhere
Thinking of you every moment I don't want to
So just fuck me and get it over with because I've got no
false pretenses
I understand what this is
And maybe I came on too strong, but I've never been one
to hold back

Personally, I sometimes prefer the delirium of a confused
and malnourished soul
What else would I do but pine over beautiful creature who
Incites madness in my heart and in my crotch
Who makes my mind so loaded
I burst with love and in my pants
Who shreds my insides with blue testicular shrapnel
Bruising my heart, the way you bruise my balls
The way you bruise my ego so disinterestedly.

I write misery
Because I am misery.

I'm a locust flower
Sprouting willow wings on the cusp of flight
Always blinking
Hoping
What I see isn't real.

There's nothing left but tear

Drops smeared across the petals of
  a flame

All echoing

    You.

Hotel Cavalier

Take me
    and i'm breathing like a dog
panting sweating brewing
up my own idea of how this goes
let's have it filthy darling, shall we?
in the front passenger seat
with your legs splayed upward and out
in those awkward looking yoga poses
you do while i'm gasping for air
watching the windows fog up
and the imprints on them become visible

faint smell of cigarettes lingering on your
hands as you run them over my face
up in between strands of hair
tongue in ear fingers gripping testes
warm clothiness rubbing against my ass
tender squeaking of suspension and
romanticized visions of endless sexcapades
endlessly coming, and coming, never going, only coming
arch of your back pierced by two dimples just above your
buttocks

immaculate marble floors, i point out to her
i don't know shit about floors.
our brown vintage luggage set was being rolled along
on a cart by some poor brown boy with strong english
through golden double doors leading to a service elevator
we took our own, found ourselves in a room full of mirrors
cautious eyes all around, dubiously caressing our bodies

and yet so sharply those eyes stung to express such frailty
that feeling of the earth trying to pull us back
as if we might have flown too far from the floor

i've got my hand buried in her hair
thick brown mane she has
massaging the back of her neck
she's wiggling her ass by then she's so excited
gently squeezing at my hand with both of hers
doors finally slide open, we're showered
by the sunlight that seems to pour
through the windows
overlooking the valley floor to ceiling
a mural drenched in sea foam green
fluorescent neon beams of electrified light
fiery clouds splashed like paint across the sky
everything beneath all of it all the people
floating about on their two clubs of flesh
that mingle with wandering sockets
who illuminate visions of distress
and of lust of hate of self loathing
of premature comings and goings
mangled in a tragic orgy of faraway gazes

she clings to my hand,
head resting on my shoulder
as i look out over that horizon
a faint smile i manage to muster
for appearances' sake
i don't give a damn
or i do and i merely feign indifference
try not to think about it too much

you've been drinking again, she says
face pressed against mine nose to nose
sniffing me out like she always does
i lightly peck her on her cheek
don't mind it darling

the drinking never ends with you,
as she walks into the bathroom.
sigh and of course i'm following

surrounded by mirrors
projections of her naked flesh
the steam rising and clouding them
slide my hand across the surface
meet my own eyes
haven't shaved in a week
i'm standing there, nude
in need of a good trim
genitals gleefully waving back at me
get into the shower with her but it's a sad sort of sensuality
a disparaging tenderness that reminds me of a mother with
a dying son
or maybe something different,
something in the way of a teardrop
falling from the lips of a kiss.

Who's Inside Me

He's got this ruffled looking mess of feathers atop his head
Like he's got so much on his mind it's bursting through His
follicles

Towering coils of black strand
Dancing orgiastically amid files
Of drumming thought relentlessly
Thumping temples of flesh

And all he can do is awkwardly smile every chance he gets
A manic on the verge of public ejaculation all the time
He's mad.

He once looked a beagle in the eyes.

Dogs must think people mad the way they look at us
All the time looking concerned or beguiled or
contemptuous

Supposedly empathetic
which says more about men than dogs.
But then again, we believe in god and dog in man
Who's who?

All the dogs of the world are out fucking casual encounters
In bars even if they don't drink but they usually do

If it isn't alcohol it's something else
Like fucking.
Looking good, he always thinks until she says she won't

Fuck him.

What about me?
He's a surgeon with his words
Until you're lying there naked
Coming under the sobering reflection
That he is not a particularly great person
To spend an evening with because like all great surgeons
He's only as good as the anesthesia he gives you.

Without it he's just a man cutting away at wounds
Until you realize how great I am at stitching them.

Hello

I thought of you today while I was out-
Side in the garden trimming the flowers
The vegetables are all starting to
Come in so beautifully
I can't wait for you to see them
It's really a sight the way the green pep-
pers look glossed over in the sunlight
The tomatoes could burst they look so succulent

It's
just so pleasing to look at the roses
The way they're starting to mingle with each-
Other; it reminds me of when we first
Met and you were this pretty little thing
That caught my eye from over yonder with
Your girlfriends smiling and giggling, me
Just standing there like some dumb oaf with his
Foot in his mouth, not sure what to say to
such a heavenly creature.

You just smiled,
And gave an awkward wave and laugh at the
strangeness of it all and this strange stranger
staring at you out over an open
field, daisies beginning to sprout up along
the sidelines. And then I didn't see you
For a long while after that until one
Night I was at this party and the cops
Shut it down. I remember walking down
One of the back roads and seeing you there

In your white lace dress, the arch of your back
visible in the moonlight, those stupid
Yellow boots you used to wear so you could
Walk home on nights like that when heels would have
Killed you.

We shared a forty on the walk
home and you were scared of me at first, but
Then we got to talking and you loosened
Up, invited me inside for some coffee.
It was the best coffee I ever had.

Sneaking onto the roof of Hotel Del
In Coronado to sneak a dip in
The pool where we stripped down to our bare flesh
And held each other in the darkness of
The water, where I got my first under-
Water blowjob and you came up gasping
For air, still laughing at the strangeness of
It all,
Still smiling, as if I'd whispered
Something charming into your ear, but all
I did was look tenderly upon your
Face because I wanted to remember
What it looked like when you realized you
Loved me.

Atmosphere

My lungs feel/Carpet soaked
Flooded Over/Blissfully Crying
Teary Eyed/Douche Fuckery
///
/////
I feel as though
My inner narrative is broken.
///
///
That needs to be fixed.
So call someone.
Who does one call?
///
Lackadaisical Lackey Lacking the

_____ _____.

I'm a pawnstar.

/////////////

Do you ever look in the mirror when you sell something
Or is it only re(ar)views.
Tell me what it means
I'll make something up,
You always do.
///
She was born with
a tail you know.
Nonononononononomono

Fingerborn.

Wetlike we like to imagine snakes.

Advancing cohesiveness,
Wet like we like to imagine snakes.

Foreboding sensibilities,
But no not really I've never been/

Spose I'll never go,
_____ _____ ___.

/

Vanity of Savages

About high-noon
Streaks of heat up between
Cracks in sun bleached leather of Earth
Salivating pools of light eucalyptus kiss
Holy highway scorched yellow line of fire
Separates dancing lotus codex flower.

Wasteful evening pre-
Seeded in celebratory banquet
Out of necessity or congratulatory envy
Obligatory gratuity
laughing madly at the way bow ties unfold
And lap dances in animal masks with glitters
Fall like jewels of night sky
Everyone tossing them aside like wild nothings.

Champagne rain golden shower stalls
Undressed eyes   flowering impulse
Shine of a shoe being kicked off
Beneath the bed
Cold whisper of the breeze
Sneaking through the blinds
Butt fucking the night away.

Do you think of me much
No not particularly, she said
Not at all
Not all but some
But not all
No not particularly

How disappointing
So is the way of life my dear
Yes but I could have married you
And I you,
But that doesn't make us markedly impressed towards
happiness
I suppose you're right, I sighed.

Counter-cultured men sitting about discussing politics
From the jaded green grass of the other side
Faded to a dying yellow
Growing into nothingness.

You know sometimes I get tired
Don't be such a droll
Followed by the sloshing of her tongue in my ear
Wondered if I must taste well.
You don't ever get tired?
Well yes, but not now
Not now?
Not now
And I knew what I had to do.

Mozart's No. 39 in E Flat Major
So hopeful, and yet
Completely inappropriate.

Cackle of the needle
Against freshly cleaned vinyl
Shiny black silhouette of sound.

Low sensual hum,
        Permeates walls.

Cigarettes to flesh
Fingertip bonfire eating up
Wooden flesh piled high
Like corpses dangling from eye full towers

I thought you said you'd quit
And you vowed you'd be faithful
Well that's not fair.
Ask me if I care.
Neither of us did, really.

Or better, neither of us do.

Infidelity's such a cold thing
How so?
What do you mean how so?
I mean it's to be expected these days
Well if it weren't for people like you
I'm not saying I condone it, but I'm not surprised by it
Then you are a foolish person without love
Maybe I'm just not blinded by it
Or maybe its absence has made you cold and dim
Possibly.

How do you know when you love someone?
You just do
That is an easy answer
I suppose it is.
Well go on then
It is a feeling similar to indigestion,
or in some cases not unlike irritable bowel syndrome.

Dark earthiness,
Soil beneath undercut nails
Elongated hair
Broken silhouettes of flesh
Pierced by endless visions

Elephants swinging their trunks
For the hell of it.

I get so fucking sick of it.
The circus,

Feels like

God I don't know know how
    to put into words

That feeling
Of stress and love
And anger
Of frustration bubbling up
Like fear bubbling in your stomach
Of bismol dreams drenched
In pinkly stomach acid.
Fucking assholes.
Self-absorbed assholes.
Cunts.

Almost lethargically the way he looks at me
I can only smile and throw up a peace sign
Cause I don't pretend to hate him
I don't even really dislike him
I just sort of find him mildly irritated

Irritating I meant to say
I'm always doing that
Always fucking up my sense of, uh...
Tense? I guess you'd call it
I dunno I'm no writer
Or maybe I am
I certainly talk about myself enough to be

You really like her don't you
She'd just say
Out of the blue
Staring up at me with glossed over marbles for eyes
Marbles quite marvelous
Pupils frayed with a crisp brown
They make me hungry
Or at least they remind me that I am.

So what's your point
They always gotta ask
Because they can't figure it out
On their own
They need to be told what it means
No one ever taught them how to think
Only to fill in bubbles and the occasional blank.

   It's not their fault
Well not entirely anyway.

When I get out of bed most mornings
I've got this terrible fucking whiskey breath
That's mixed with that after stench of vomit
and cigarette smoke
and whatever else I indulge in

I used to wonder how they'd kiss me
Then I realized it's because I was somehow better
Than the last guy
'Somehow' is a dubious word
I should have said
Because I am
better
Or at least I keep telling myself.

I would rather lick bloody fucking cunt again
Than sit down with these people.

These banquets
So obnoxiously over the top.

Twat

You've always had this rusty colored face
that shines with the glazing of your skin
with the fractals of the light bouncing about
like the neurons of the brain
against fleshy white walls of padding
beginning to fade to that dingy yellow

the way teeth do when you forget to brush
or when they've dried overnight
because you're no longer salivating
from all the amphetamines you've done
and so your mouth overflows with ash
and soggy white jisms flaking
over dried skin of lips.

Nights spent ravaged and horny
willing to bribe a stripper you like for sex
she was cheaper than you expected
but you think that's because she likes you
which isn't the worst thing in the world
she's cute an all, but one has to wonder
how many other guys like you she fucked
for a hundred an fifty bucks.

It was good though you're always
thinking about something else
your mind is always
somewhere
else.

At first
it was pretty great because
ya know
you'd take forever to come
but after a while
it sort of saps you
of the enjoyment
so it gets
to be

What's the point?

You take immense pleasure
in food maybe even more than sex
which is saying something since
you men are all such sex obsessed fiends.

Anyways you really enjoy
good food you love
a good meal sitting down

the whole act of preparation
both preparation to cook
and to eat

the whole process is
very ritualistic and inviting to you
and so when you invite someone
to eat with you it's a very intimate thing

because you're a savage when you eat
not that you can't restrain yourself which you do
when the occasion necessitates but really

you just go out and it's not uncommon
for bits of food to fall out of your mouth
sometimes projected and for you to go on
as if nothing happened

because in your mind
  nothing did happen
which in itself is not unusual.

You spend a lot of time
thinking
about writing
before you actually get any done.

It's as if you've got to
let the thought marinate
before you can cook it

sous vide diction
deliciously succulent medley of words—

I like what the kid puts out
but there's too much sex and the swearing.

But then you used to dislike Kerouac
because you thought he was overly sentimental

which he is
but that isn't the crime of the writer
it's the crime of humanity
the same humanity he writes about
with honesty authenticity

Point is... *I* really fucking like Kerouac
now that I've gotten older.

Suppose maybe I'll like what this kid
has to offer down the road
as my tastes or his work matures.

You wish you could write every day
or at least during the day
you've never been able to write in daylight
or at least anything good.

You used to worry about coming off as egotistical
but that notion has long left you
even though it's exactly how you're seen
but then what, should you go around
pretending you're awful

cause I don't think you should
how can you expect anyone to think you're good
if you don't even think you're good
and don't give me that *there has to be a balance...* shit
because that's a farce
and I don't believe in that
I believe in honesty

In the writing anyway.

He's polite but you can smell the confidence lingering
beneath his skin,

I've never liked long lines.

It's not that you don't think he's good
you just hate that he knows he's good
and the irritating part is
he probably thinks you're jealous of him
probably cause you are but just the fact that he knows it
really pisses you off.

I love symmetry,
just not in my architecture.

Prayer

Painfully sounding off locomotive rhythms
whistled rimes
Woefully incompetent   malignant Christ
offering's slim

Can't comprehend that self-destructive nature
in itself, righteousness and wickedness and whatnot.
Try tellin' pop you aint' heard that one before.

Prayin' for better days.
Play it loud, that's what the sticker on the front says
Read it,

Play It Loud

Words themselves beaten like worn tambourines and
broken huaraches
Stapled shut the way mouths staple hearts to clouts of
inscrutable madness.
Cathartic human feast, still waiting for better days.

All thanks to God,
an old woman says to herself, accented.
arriving home at midnight after a double shift
at the hospital cleaning rooms, cleaning death, cleaning up
after sickness.

Told her not to thank God, but you.
She thanks God and then you.

She'll always thank God before she thanks you.

Les Girls

My brother took me to my first strip club
I wasn't very old, just maybe eighteen
and there's this bright half burnt-out sign
out front that says

Les Girls

pink neon letters
flashing twenty feet above me
and there's a sex shop next to it,
I forget the name
anyway

we stop in the store first
because there's time to kill
ornamental pornography adorned the walls like jewels
hallways of smut stretching on in the distance

I get to looking around the shop
and there are all sorts of things
I didn't even know about,
alien sex dolls, horse-skin condoms

it made me laugh
because suddenly
I didn't feel
so strange
about my own
minor fetishes that
I'm sure everyone has

or hides or both

I thought about what my girl'd say if I brought home a
vibrator for her
shaped like a big throbbing cock,
vein an all

such a conservative girl
no I take that back she's
my little sweet tart

she wants it more than
I do half the time

not that that's bad
I mean
what guy ever complains
about too much sex
honestly

but seriously, my cock is beat.

my brother buys
five DVDs
for ten bucks
cause there's a sale

so he puts em' in my car
by then the club's open
girl's standing at the door

smiling with that
porcelain looking smile of hers

lingerie clinging to her body

my brother
half mad half in love already
with her
while I quietly smile to myself

He can be so willful
in his naivety sometimes
even though he's the one
introducing me to life's
great pleasures.

I get to a cage
with a desk behind it

the girl gives me a ticket
that I give to the girl
standing next to me
who stamps my hand

the stamp glows in the dark
it's of a woman with large breasts
in that cartoony sort of way

like Jessica Rabbit
chest bulging out and whatnot

by then I'm pretty excited myself
except that it's a Wednesday night

so the first girl to step out
looks to be in her second trimester I think

or maybe worse, she *actually* is,
which makes me feel even more perverse

I get to thinkin' about people
with their peculiar inclinations

ya know like
everything that's on the internet these days
not to sound like an old guy
cause I'm not...not yet anyways

horse-fucking, goose-fucking, elderly pregnant women,
bisexual threesomes, mature male foursomes, two-girls one
cup, one man one jar, pain olympics, incest cousin fuckers

honestly
it's a bit overwhelming
how particular people are
when it comes to getting off.

second girl came up
an italian braud
in'er early forties
shakin' her ass
with such enthusiasm

I had to tip her, so I did
and my brother turns to me
lightly slaps my shoulder

you don't have to tip them
because you feel sorry for them
you'll be broke in an hour if you do

and avoid eye contact

why?
because that's how they get ya!

by the third hour the lineup had started over
so we agreed we'd both get lap dances and head out
my brother paid for mine and I chose the 5th or 6th girl
I forget, but her name was Missy and she was a great dancer

I remember I get out to that cage I bought my ticket from
an I says I'd like to have Missy for three songs, please
lady let out a small laugh at how childish I must have
sounded

Missy comes in an' sort of jokingly yells,
hey you wanna' fuck in the booth in the theatre?
Missy was funny

And a great dancer.

Feels Like Hooverville

Rag doll mercy the way
you've got your pins
and fucking
needles in me

making me dance
the way you'd dance with fireflies
beneath almond colored faces
bleached with stony grimaces
who's repetitious

over and over
        and over and over
                    and over and over
stabbed me
in the ears with endless cuckery
and cockles
tickling my underflesh
with such painful pleasantry

you're a hippo
 you're a hippo
  you're a hipp
oh.

it makes less sense when you put it what way
but I still see your point even though
you don't have one

don't wander unless I tell you to.

you stink like fuck-sweat
and pussy oils
which is strange considering

I always loved the way pussy breathes.

quit showboating.
now you're just over-
thinking?
I meant compensating,

but it's practically the same thing.

Hoffman's Triumph

Watching someone do drugs, watching the mind begin to slip and slur, their thoughts bouncing off the walls of their consciousness like loose echoes reverberating back and forth between two players on a court, is a terribly dull thing to watch. But then I've never been a person of the rationale that you can get a lot higher without drugs than with them. Focus on the object. Focus on the target. Think about it. What changed? It didn't seem so strange at first, but now that you notice it there's a little girl on a scooter riding towards you in the dark whistling some old tune you'd heard somewhere before. She's far enough that you can't make her face, but her figure's there and it's rolling on toward you even though she never seems to actually get any closer. That old tune, like something you'd sing Yankee Doodle to, travelling through the space between your ears and the time it takes to do it. Starts to feel real, the way the sirens ring out and clash against the sky. Cymbals in a drumline being struck together like matches being lit. Beams of light that shoot through the moonlit fognight, percolating in those transient morning mists, illuminate bits of the pathway as I walk along the tree line. Towering hedges glaring over my shoulder as I walk by, anxiously, quickly but with a-

*Throw up.

Puke splashed across the walkway, take a seat on the curb, light a cigarette and think about what you've done. What you've done. What you've done.
Sit there, letting your feet dangle off the edge. That

street's so far down now. Wonder how far that drop is?
How deep? Take a step forward, don't leap, just let yourself
go. No falling, only being, let what will, being what is. Look
up at the edge as it falls away from you, or maybe rises. You
don't really know which way, you just know you're going
that way. Go that way. Go a way. Go away. Think about it.
Not too hard, you'll have an aneurysm. Don't fight it. Feel
it. Touch it. Let it finger your thoughts with that tenderness
you hide behind your reticence. The bottom's so bright.
Maybe it's the top, doesn't feel like the top, but it's not what
I expected either way. I'm not quite walking, but it sure as
hell takes some effort to get from here to there. Coordinate
the movements. You can actually see yourself behaving in
this terrible fashion. Legs beginning to buckle, both fighting
to step first. Arms outstretched with open palms, reaching
out for something, maybe a rail to lean on. Cold click of a
heel to the concrete steps you're climbing. See that light
flickering just above that old Ford? It reminds me of a
picture I saw once where these kids are standing next to a
rusted truck. The window panes are broken, back when they
used real glass. There's no wheels on it. Just tall blades of
grass growing in through the floorboard and the mountains
in the background are standing over the three of them, as if
it's their job or maybe they just like to sit and stare like
elders on a porch not quite waiting for anything but maybe
death. Mom and Dad. They're both sitting there shaking
their heads, pointing their fingers. letting the words fall
from their mouths. Little blemishes of sound trying to climb
through my eyes cause my ears are clogged with all these
colors in their rush to get in. 405 jam. Slow to a crawl.
Parents still talking, still trying to tell me something. My lip
is quivering but when I look at my reflection it seems to be
kissing my face. It's just so damn in love with itself. Look at

that face, those beautiful brown eyes. They're these great orbs of not-quite flesh, but maybe something more important. Little capsules for the soul. Dilate. Soul release. Uncage the animal. Make a beast of yourself. When did you stop apologizing? Around the same time you stopped trying to remember what day it was except to know if the liquor store was closing early tonight. It wasn't. Not like it matters though, well it did, but it doesn't now. Not when it's late enough to get up for work. Not like you're going to work. It'll pass, I hope. Probably won't. Maybe it will. Yes, it most certainly will. Mom and Dad won't let this one go methinks. I'm used to that. I can handle that. Don't make this about you. This is about me. I'm the one who doesn't have a problem. Remember? Take a seat, keep eye contact. Strong eye contact, don't break away, even for a second. You're unhinged. You're seconds away from going postal just so you don't have to look at those tired, worn out caricatures that seem so bent on being persistent. But the words aren't as bad as you ever imagine they will be. Maybe you're genuinely sorry when you say it, at least for that moment, but the seconds go by and you've convinced yourself you've done nothing wrong. You're not sure why it's wrong, but you know it is wrong. Wouldn't be the only thing. Slide out of them blue jeans, foot getting caught in the hole by the knee as you do. Feel that air, chilly, delicately fondling your genitals. Look at that hair, it's so curly. He'll die with a full head of hair, I just know it. I just know it.

Touch

Manifestations of preordained gesticulations of madness
  And I'm standing there looking at this faceless figure
And he waves to me from out the silhouette of the wall
  And I say why you lookin at me like that way?
               But he gets it so he laughs
    and he walks across the ceiling to the door
          And I'm hanging upside down by my hair
only it's tied to the knob
          And the heat's beginning to pick up and
the hinge starts to warm
          And my soup's getting cold but I drink it
anyways or eat it or whatever
          And my socks have holes in them and my
underwears are faded black
          And my asshole bleeds from the
hemorrhoids when I wipe my shit
          And my eye sockets are sunken craters
bathed in purple
          And my cock is hard cause I aint had any
in a while
          And I think about love and I toss the
thought aside
          And I wail about drunk and stupid and
naked and writhing
          And I forget to go do that thing I was
s'posed to do anyhow
          I start to finger the thought of
benevolence but I give up on it
          And I whisper dirty words that slink into
his ear, fondling his ego

        And I'm hungry so I ask for some food,
at least I think I did
or he didn't hear me
        And I get up bare-ass naked walk to the
kitchen burn my hand on the stove
        And I put some ice on it but I'm hungry
so I forget about it
        But there it is again and I'm staring at
him and he's smiling
        Through that thick veil of darkness that
seems to ring out in pleasure to me
        What's hiding in there I might think if I
weren't so lazy about that sort of thing
        Or maybe I just don't care that God
might not have created us
        Or he did and I just don't mean much to
him anyways
        Or something else like life's just a prelude
to eternity
        Or you spend all your time dead so waste
your time alive

An I get to wondering when I'll die
  So I says to God
I says
  God...
Cause I don't patronize him like those God
awhmighty types do
An I says
  I realize if I die young
 If I were to die now, at this point in my life
 It's my own fault.
I deserve it.

[69]

But
An I hold my finger up
   But, smiling as I say it
now is not the time.
    I wait for him to laugh but there is no response
   Other than the throngs of frogs blurping loudly
beneath the cover of darkness and grass
So I slouch forward
And wonder how long I've got

And again I strip down naked pacing the room
  Or I'm walking on molten rocks with smiling faces
And I'm looking back down on them and they're so sterile
  And there's smoking drifting off the tips of my fingers
Filling the room with transient mists of ghostly apparitions
  And I'm telling myself it's alright, it's alright
because I realize what's happening
  Until someone else joins the conversation but I can't find
them
I can't find the source of the voice until it becomes evident
  Until I've kissed him goodnight
I'm waving to the mirror as it shatters
And the shards of glass rain down
Cutting me until there's nothing left.
  But there's a picture of a sunset
in my mind
  Atop a hill on a warm evening
When the breeze isn't so stiff
And picture after picture slides behind my eyes
With the click of a thought
And I've been to the ends of badlands
Through the frozen bowels of glaciers
  Through the torrential gales of hurricanes

Across the petrified remains of fallen cities
And one prevailing thought makes itself known

I have lived a beautiful life.

I Am a Cancerous Nothing

I am Nothing
 Have done Nothing
   Love Nothing
That's a lie,

    Because
        I've been in love all my life.

I am infectiousness
Lingering about the sole
Spiritual sores adorning the soul
Sorely missing the point
Never feigning so,
Only mellowing in barrels brimmed with ignorance.

Annoying ignorance
Childlike temperament.

Oh
god, how I would kill to

That's not right is it,
So why do it?

It's not as if

    All I ever wanted was to be a
Stop talking.

You must really like to hear yourself speak.

Stop talking,

   You club me
Stalking top.

I am a foolish man,
To have thought otherwise.

      But she a foolish woman,
For some reason I can't think of,
  I am dead.

Ode To Parkinson's

I sat alone
In the darkness of the morning fog
And I lit a cigarette.
It felt much too thin between the tips of my fingers.
Smoke trailed off
Copulating with the breaths of emergent vapor.
My hand stayed steady, momentarily,
Giving in to the uncontrollable urge of movement.
I watched my fingers tremble
With a mind of their own
As if belonging to someone else.
Maybe they did.

Life is a Calloused Vein Refusing to Bleed Out

Eyes bleed out of calloused skull
Way my mime mimes lifeter looking forward with disease.
And all I can think about is that cocked smile bent
Like your crooked heart bends me to your whim.
Would it be more pleasing if I told you nature was worth
expediating?

Six thousand times six thousand reasons
I'm an evolutionary nebula choking on missionary
But narcissism becomes dull,

The same way life, and eventually
You get dull.

Thoughts left on the cutting room floor
Are probably the most endearing to human nature.
It is
For this reason I believe in dreams
Their honesty coupled with that divine loss of sanity
Glamorized by romantics and scorned by those in a
perpetual state
Of inherent nervousness.
Fingers dancing like needles stumbling to balance
Falling over themselves as they walk across flesh.

There's no point to it, people say
Always whining about futility.

What about now? What about this or that
Whatever floats your boat etcetera etcetera.
Because now, we're getting somewhere.
That smile forming on the corners of your lips,
That stifled breathing as you feel your tells telling everything
I'll never have to ask if only I'd look
And see dilated pupils honestly interested.
Bring a smile to my heart,
I'll take a knife to yours.

Amnesiac

IcanIcan
  sense something strstrange about thisis plaace.
I'veev'I neeb ereh erofeb
  I meanttneam
What I mean is is what I mean

            Is.

    I've got piss on my
short   s.

blakblancblanckblackblank

  What did you say?

Sigh-
    -lense ing grate ing

  Were'dsewn to gather

Get your face out of my skin.

Ica an since some things strain age
  sense something about the
his plays.
I believe I need arab arafat
  I mint t uhm
What I mean is is what I mean

            Is

Wait, what?

Why Did I Come in Here?

IcanIcan
   sense something strstrange about thisis plaace.
I'veev'I neeb ereh erofeb
   I meanttneam
What I mean is is what I mean

                  Is.

      I've got piss on my
short   s.

blakblancblanckblackblank

   What did you say?

Sigh-
      -lense ing grate ing

   Were'dsewn to gather

Get your face out of my skin.

Ica an since some things strain age
   sense something about the
his plays.
I believe I need arab arafat
   I mint t uhm
What I mean is is what I mean

                  Is

Wait, what?

See Right Through You

I'm sleeping
Or at least it feels that way
As I stare outwardly

Overlooking the sterile linoleum room
Pale palette of blue hues adorned with
The faces of smiling children learning to
Manage their diabetes or their asthma

And I can actually hear the bubbling
Sensation from my lungs
That I'm here for now,

Every time I exhale.

I can feel it
In the bottom of my left lung,
Like a can being scraped against pavement
I already know, and for the first time
In months I want a cigarette

I'm smiling and laughing about it to myself because
Isn't that typical.

My reflection in the mirror is pale and gaunt with
Purple under sagging brows puffed lids
And all that reflection can do is sleepily stare inward
Lazily, not quite afraid, but perpetually daydreaming
Wondering if maybe he himself is a creation of
Someone's clouded thoughts.

Like blood smeared across his face he's
Blush where just below the surface of his skin
He doesn't realize it yet, but
That feeling
's beginning to make itself known.

She comes in holding a folder
Pulls em out, holds em to the light
Sitting there back half bent
He quietly says hello
As she says goodbye,
But not before placing a compassionate hand
And a disheartened expression, barely concealed
indifference.

Can't blame her.
Wonder how many people she tells the same thing to
Every day of her life.

I bet she wanted to make a difference
when she took this job.

Weak End with Mom

Do you have to be reminded
of absent kicks in gut, or turning in belly
The nauseating fear of   ?

Toads don't play leap-frog.

Mimosas in the morning before we takes them to school,
ice breakers on breath
Daddy- it's just orange, juice me cause I'
m dried up like falay salmon, dried up like persistence stays
persistent
On school day mornings hangin over limp without no-
reason
Double negative the way I like my tests in the bathroom,
Wait the smiley face is bad, never mind tryna stay limp like
my spirit lies lazy.

Periods belong at the end of sentences.

At the end of months should be celebratory,
But there's only other months, other days, endless until they
end
                    Noticed that thing you do with the
rhythm of your voice
Quivered like we first met in Sunday school while mom
watched eagerly
That we might love in the name of god, but I don't know
his name so how
Do you miss what you never knew? or at least you never
met the guy, so

How do you know

Bloody Mary three times in the rearview mirror, watching
her
Jog behind trying to keep up w hile the laughter echoes as if
thoughts linger
Parasitically. You're impressed with light I see, but   's
only fingerless lust fingering about the cords on jacket,
driving through crowded intersection loud waving loud
waving loud weaving loud wailing loaded

Question

        's lead only to more answers.
Don't tell her I told you not to tell her.

Have a good weekend, honey.
        Bye.

Lullaby

Sometimes you've got to sit with it a long while,
entire nights spent lolling about in lethargy,
dreaming of that sunrise

That sticks to morning clouds,
no not necessarily dreaming, not enough asleep for that
but it feels as though you're looking through warped glass at
everything from far away.

I wish there were a word for that feeling of uncertainty that
permeates your heartbeat
arch of the back so slight,

       Tyranny/ Jubilee copulate madly.

There sitting on a park bench is a man in a black trench coat
with a gun to his head,
nothin but a fellow there to tell him stop, an he does but
that's not important.

          I never killed a man before, but I thought
of it, only regret the boy.

Forget about home for a while.

I
like to watch old films while   I   ,
      Not always old. Old enough.

      I'd really hoped I wouldn't die.

I'd really hoped I wouldn't die.

But here, falling from clocktowers are plot twists
I hadn't foreseen

The tyranny of the left margin weighs about as
much as a gram of rice soaked in gallons of rubbing alcohol.
If there is a God, he's smiling down on the drunks
he lets die beside railroad tracks as they stumble home,
falling asleep beneath pouring rain, barechested and alive
and then so quickly of exposure,

Decimate me gently.

So I can drearily drift along the cusp of
wild(er)ness,
Of testicular fortitude, and pulmonary grace.

Shallow like my breath,
like your eyes when they see me ddribbling
madness out of cooked spoons in bathroom stalls
locomotive heart chugging along,

Chugging until blackness,
until ocifers of the law find you swollen like
overripe plum, drizzling life filtered out unto oblivion. Big
talk for a man who's dead, I thought

Until he said a word,
made me shudder. Swollen lips to match. Wrinkled fingers
the way his thoughts crumpled like paper drenched in ,
broken methodology.

We were friends until I killed myself. Or maybe it was him
first. Enlightenment is overwhelming at time.
I say time because there is no separateness in the delineating
narrative,

                              I is also loosely tossed about.

It seems like there's an acute awareness of the scientific
throes of death, reeling time's line.
Would you fuck a ,

                    Prince if you knew he was a pig?
                        [Space]

Arrogant hopelessness-   lathered with digression, leg
room   I like that you labeled it.
I don't care that you liked it I like that I liked it I liked that
space   leaves so much room for thought
the way digging does   have you ever had to dig holes
for a living? It could drive a man mad the way it leaves so
much room for thought   let a man think about the
blisters forming beneath the skin of his calloused hands and
eventually he'll cut them off   hoping for some
tranquility   am I talking about two or three or all
men when I recollect eyes deadening with sunrise that
seems to shoo away morning mist ferry of

           [Substitute for Soul]------------------It went that way

I used to believe in the goodness of men, because when I
would look into their eyes all I saw was a radiant pigment
calibrating to the tenderness of my being,
Flawed gems are still flawed.

However worthless they may be they're still interesting to observe, or at least you hope you can get something out of them.

I've
got a seven hour
record on repeat and
all I can think about is
if it'll last long enough
for eternity. Sing us
through the
intermediary,

I'm not done
with the way shapes
shift, just yet I've still
got that train, that
bullet, that drink to
catch. Snarl with some
feeling as
I/you/he/she/we,
well you know.

I'm
starting to
realize why I
never had any
friends.

Marigold

The neighborhood cat's been preaching again
That raspy smokers croak he has
Scratches the ear with thoughtful
Pieces of meat to chew on
When you're lying in bed trying to masturbate
As the sun rises.

Stifled breaths with each stroke
Trying to picture those gorgeous tits bouncing up down
Straddling your cock with her butterfaced mouth
Stoney looking eyes puffed red Monarch
Kissing south for the early riser.

Licking like fire licks the underside of mantles
With warmth and intimacy intended
Burning instead.

Ride and she rides again,
Head thumping against the wall with each pelvis
Inching closer and closer six inches closer
A half-foot bone without a bone
Somehow broken in the way the spirit wanes under pressure
In the way pricks lie dormant under spotlights.

                                mother,

Kissing lavender,
Brings thoughts of flowers instead of crude sex
And honey,
Tastes sweetly innocent.

Watering the mangled marigold blooming prematurely
Bright blossom delicately unfolding
Looming over dirt with apprehensive eyes for sun

Illuminate.

What a Sad Little Man

I thought.
he had these thick thighs
carrying the weight of his bulbous belly
real pale looking
a bit like an orchid
i almost expected him to die should he uproot himself
he sat on a bench in the park surrounded by ducks
that were all too scared to take bread crumbs
from him and his face betrayed a sense of hurt.

I whistled as i walked along the stony path
only i'm not very good at whistling
my lips are always chapped and flaking
but that's alright because there are worse things
in life than dry lips,
or at least in some people's lives.

Dark rain clouds clung to the sky
dusty looking cotton candy balls
a light sprinkle, but no real rain
and that sad little man was looking
up towards the sky, maybe for an answer
but probably just for rain or lightning,
his hand was propped against his head
to keep his cap from falling off,
and i thought about what his head might look like.

I could feel the chill of the concrete through my shoe
holes in the heel and the toe on my left and right foot
respectively, irritatingly.

When i sat down on the bench next to him
his face
turned, towards me.
Stone-like eyes filled with grief.

I smiled awkwardly, nervously laughing.

How's it going,
Weather's not too great today.
No it isn't, he said. But then it never is.

I felt uncomfortable.

How old are you, he asked.
You look a lot like my son.
I'm twenty.
And I am.

My Usual Languor

There's a portraiture about your face that reminds me
I used to be such a story teller. Only now I'm sitting
Beneath canvassed overages constantly reminding me
I'm probably over the hill,

What with everything that's going on.

I don't like to swear anymore because it reminds me
Of a time when it meant something to use words before
It came to the revelatory exclamations of defamatory
Linguistics. I used to believe in the permeance and the
Permanence,

How's it feel, lingering onward among nostalgia.

Days used to be ladies splayed open like cadavers but
Now they're never pierced by dull blades of wordsmith.
I might have liked that rhythmic repetition you have
It's worn out the way your welcome is.

Someone's got to discuss your affairs before you're gone.
It'll be me planning my own procession, carrying myself
The way I've always been carried by others.

It doesn't feel that way anymore.
I wish it   did.
Words thinning with   hair,

I wish very few things.

If You'd Close the Door, You'll Never Have to See the Day Again

I'm so fucking hungover.

I'm falling out of bed languid and embalmed
Scowling at post-modernism   Dropping deuces on the
queen's portrait
Buy the liquor at the liquor store from my Iranian friend
Majid who sells me cigarettes at cost I buy so much liquor
from him
Smiles   Yellow porcelain must comb his teeth
with butter
Smile at me flicking ash off end of cigarette
Sidewalk clicks beneath heels tramping down apartment
roadway
Stumble at the light for switch that tells go   Honk of
horns and angry fists
Put your cock away   Pissing on birds

Birds don't stay still long enough to piss on,
But they did   and I did   Ass screaming pain
Stinking hemorrhoids ought to burst
Way my dreams burst all over her ugly face
She'd kick me in the groin to tell me how ugly I am
Kicks with her crotch.

My cock is drooling.

And she...the longtime cock smoker itching for her fix
Is about to get it again, only maybe I ask her to choke me
I'm tired of merely ramming it into her   I don't even bother
to come anymore
Boredom tolerates me   Until our hands wrap around
each other's necks
Wildly thrusting, the blood beneath her lips quietly
coagulating
Pale blue, color of overcast skies and her skin

Angular flesh the way hills roll over each other
Time bleeding into itself indifferently
Outside the bedroom window raindrops sing
Complacency of cold weather is oddly attractive to me
Awaken at night to pull her closer to me,
stifled breath against my chest

I am the cold air waiting to consume you.

All Good Men

All good men are of me
All good men are droplets of sweat excreting themselves
from my pores

The goodness I expel
All good men sprout themselves from the seed of my being
through the dirt of my flesh
From the womb of my mind
Like dark matter children, anti-matter beings in a state of
cathartic sympathy

Good men are like children plucked from the orphanage of
my stature
I am the stonefaced exuberance of moralistic-reverse-
osmosis
Pray for me,

Apparently, I need it.
That is what you people do, right?

From my well goodness is drawn
And made to love
Making love

All that is good
Is of me.

Frailty

Trembling hands with long bony fingers
Dirt sitting just beneath the nails
Extended outward
Catching formerly occupied
Space.
Stringy hair coils down forehead
Jet black - patches of gray - stray reds
Loose looking skin clings to
Gaunt cheek
Bones jutting out
Like limbs of a willow tree
Trying to catch itself from
Falling.
Faint smell of ammonia
Of that elderly residue that
Lingers beneath blanketed
Thought
Plastered over newspaper
Wallsofabeautifulmind
Crumbling under weight
Less
Eyes pouring out
Souls to anyone with a goblet
Able and welling
With dried tears being
Packaged like apricots
Salted like Earth
Buried like bodies
Egotistically absent
Faces

Smiling wide and toothy
Flush with hopefulness
Crying aloud with conjectures
Of enlightenment
And absent minded professors
Of blood red eyes
And golden haired
Boys
Speaking as if spoken to
Here I am,
Waiting
to embrace you.

Portrait of a Portrait

I almost believe that coy smirk smiling back at me

That dubious looking self-portrait hung up

On solitude and the wall

Paisley tapestry papering behind

Lingering botanical thoughts

Brought about by some primordial sense of

The Earth drenched in envious moss

Golden Green swelling over

Edge of water murky enough

To be clear it's flowing

Backwards in haste

Inward. Inward.

Fuuuuuuuuuuuuuuuuuck.

I thought

I remembered

Her name

Butt

It escapes me.

The ashtray

Held ashes of

Friends always try

To kill you

Always try

To love you

To death.

Heart is a Withered Plant Wounded by Words

I can't think about it right now
I've got a masturbatory muscle memory that cramps up
Every time I get a hard-on.
Makes wishful thinking a little less dissatisfying.
Hand hurts though;
Starts in the thumb, movement becomes restrained
Spreads through the palm of the hand to the index
To the middle, to the ring

And now you've got a useless writing hand.

Palette on the ground covered in dried up paints
Inkling to shit moving through my bowels towards my
asshole.
There's faint sound of music playing dreamily through the
walls
I slam my broken fist against   screaming
obscenities
Broken plates of breakfast splattered over canvas, walls,
Heart-   Worn and shredded   Way clothes lie
tattered and ruined.

No mister post man, I don't think I'll see you tomorrow.
But you don't know that   I'm leaving.
Too tired too proud to drearily persist, merely.

I'm an empirical illusion,
An observational empire

Built on the premise that what you see you can believe,
That the uniformity of natural laws will persist as they
always have.

Feels out of place,
But then that might be the point.
Eyes are habitual-
When they lie, when they cheat, when they love, when they
fuck
Habit overcomes them.

I've got the same problem,
Only I'm too afraid to admit it.

L'Appel Du Vide

   Silence grates my ears like
nickel plated screws through cheese grater
Funny looking gait of man's nose, next to me
smiling placidly stupidly
Snaggle toothed grin smugly irreverent. I smell lysol on his
skin sticking like
Tobacco particles of the third hand. If I could light a
cigarette from the spark of his eyes I would
Start a burning pit in the heart of this house where rugs
chairs picture frames piled high would
Illuminate the dark candlemissed corners of the house.
   If I could offer this anonymous group of twats a drink I'd
smile bracingly as everything collapsed
Around me a gown dressed in debris frowning with delight
a broken tract imploding in itself. Was
There even a replacement of sound? Could silence tangibly
confess its irritant qualities its confessional tendency to illicit
mad screams of jubilee hysterical laughter melting through
gaping electrical crevice opening wide and hard and staring
with posterity at posteriors pestering hypoxic do-goods
doing no good. Eyes lolling back to skulls licking at lines-
anonymity succumb-
   "Brandon? Do you have anything to see?" You mean-
   "Anything to say at all?" Heart's like broken phonograph-
broken speaker blown out muffling familiar sounds
fornication of familiarity and sonicological abscess. I'm
silent because even to say no is to say something.
   Without stairs without stares without stayers we thought
prayers we are stairs staring upwardly at the absent
iridescent light longing for an absolute tense- longing for

the fulfillment of absence in the way it empties out lockets
of love and personality.
You've lost
It all comes down to the magnitude of that foot tapping that
stopped fifteen minutes ago in the reflection of judgmental
eyes feigning absence. Deadening ring growing like
thumping heart blood squirting through arterial passage
deadening heart deadening sight ocular occurrence of
aqueous forms finagling cataracts all maligning my impotent
spirit my important spite spitting on the shiny shoed feet
laid out before me in circular conveyance. Scream.

About the Author

Brian Strauss is the author of *Call of the Void* and *Strung Like Puppets*. Raised in Chula Vista since 1993–he resides in San Diego with his cat Rogelio.